While the piece is composed of simple and clearly defined elements, they are integrated in such a seamless and natural way that the whole is by far greater than the individual parts. And as such, it's actually hard to do the piece justice by describing the elements that when interweaved make it so brilliant.

Theatre is Easy

... this off Broadway production ... offers you the same heartfelt journey of any multi-Tony award winning storytelling piece of theatre. Tin Bucket Drum *is a mesmerizing piece of Kabuki style African storytelling.*

The Examiner

So cohesive in artistic vision is this piece that it is decidedly difficult to parse out responsibility for its success.

The New York Theatre Review

In a theater world full of high-flying superheroes and next-level spectacles, Tin Bucket Drum *charmingly reminds us that, ultimately, what matters most is the story.*

The Village Voice

A timeless story with universal appeal, one that Ben Okri and George Orwell could have written if they had put their heads together.

The Star

Dedicated to Pumzile Gumede

Tin Bucket Drum

Neil Coppen

WITS UNIVERSITY PRESS

Published in South Africa by:
Wits University Press
1 Jan Smuts Avenue
Johannesburg, 2001
www.witspress.co.za

First published 2016
978-1-86814-972-8 (print)
978-1-86814-973-5 (PDF)

Application to perform this work in public and to obtain a copy of
the play should be made to: Dramatic, Artistic and Literary Rights
Organisation (DALRO), P O Box 31627, Braamfontein, 2017. No
performance may be given unless a licence has been obtained.

Edited by Pat Tucker
Proofreader: Tanya Paulse
Cover image: aisle_B with thanks from UJ Arts & Culture
Cover design: Michelle Staples
Typesetting: Quba Design, South Africa
Printed and bound by Creda, South Africa

Contents

Acknowledgements

Thank you to actress Ntando Cele who originated the role and contributed immeasurably to realising this story on the stage; as well as to the extraordinary percussive input of Wake Mahlobo who devised the original score and toured with the production for over a decade. Thank you too to the production's original director Karen Logan, actress Mpume Mthombeni and stage-manager Nosipho Bophela – all of whom have ensured this story has been seen and heard in theatres around the world.

Further thank you to: Sam de Romijn of the Imbewu Trust, Thuli Zuma, Margie Coppen of Think Theatre, Mike Mazzoni, Ismail Mahomed, Kate Axe–Davies, The National Arts Festival team, Xavier Vahed, Val Adamson, Jesse Kramer, George Holloway, Christine Skinner, Bryan Hiles, Mike Broderick, Colwyn Thomas, Angella and Greg Coppen, Jade Bowers, Adrienne Sichel, Dylan McGarry, cover designer Michelle Staples, Roshan Cader and the Wits University Press team, and Vaughn Sadie.

Foreword

Ismail Mahomed
Artistic Director
National Arts Festival (South Africa)

When Neil Coppen won the 2011 Standard Bank Young Artist Award he shared a heart-warming anecdote from his childhood in which he tells of a wooden puppet theatre his father built for him when he was eight years old. Using it to tell stories for pocket money at children's birthday parties became a stepping stone to a career that has made him one of South Africa's most celebrated young playwrights.

Coppen's strength lies in his remarkable talent for telling stories through the voices of characters whose lives are richly textured by the personal and the political. He never lowers the tone to become didactic. He never raises it so high it becomes a sermon. He never makes it so unreal that it becomes unbelievable.

It is probably for this reason that *Tin Bucket Drum* (2005) and *Tree Boy* (2010), earned him the prestigious Standard Bank Young Artist Award and led to his commissioned work, *Abnormal Loads* (2011). At the National Arts Festival in Grahamstown, *Tin Bucket Drum* and *Tree Boy* played alongside at least 300 other productions and it would have been easy for the work of a new, young playwright to get lost in a vast programme where popular and established names pull the crowds. However, thanks to Coppen's early experience as a storyteller and his ability to weave together elements of magic realism, shadow puppetry, Afro-Kabuki and live percussion, *Tin Bucket Drum* rose to the surface and stood out as one of the gems of the Fringe.

Since then *Tin Bucket Drum* has earned standing ovations and critical reviews from Grahamstown to Cape Town and New York. At the 2007 Musho Festival in KwaZulu-Natal the play won the Audience Vote Award. At the 2010

National Arts Festival it was honoured with the Standard Bank Fringe Ovation Award. When it opened in New York it received glowing reviews, proving that Coppen's work resonates both with audiences and with critics beyond geographical and cultural boundaries.

In *Tin Bucket Drum* Coppen takes the reader and audience into Tin Town, a village ruled by a dictator who makes life unbearable for his subjects. It is here, in this drought-affected village, that the remarkable Nomvula and her mother try to find a better future. Unbeknown to them their new home is dominated by an official who attempts to keep the inhabitants in their place by imposing on them the rule of silence. Coppen gives this official the unceremonial name, Censor.

While Tin Town may be in a 'different' world that even the smartest GPS could not pinpoint, it is also a village that exists everywhere in the Americas, Europe, Asia and Australia as much as it exists in Africa. It is only through using the rhythms of the African style of storytelling that Coppen allows us to imagine Tin Town as a village in Africa.

Tin Town is a metaphor for our current political situation. It could be the Zuma presidential compound, Nkandla, as much as it could be the rest of South Africa. The Censor could be the parliamentary Bill that that seeks to control information. We, the citizens of South Africa, who have kept in office a president with so many human weaknesses, could be the apathetic inhabitants of Tin Town. Could the rising young voices that are increasingly speaking out against the status quo be Neil Coppen's young girl, Nomvula, whose passionate heartbeat cannot be silenced?

Or could Tin Town be in Zimbabwe? Or in George Bush's America? Or Gadaffi's Libya? Or in Syria? Israel? Pakistan?

Tin Town is everywhere. It is a global village. As more youth-driven movements across the globe make their voices heard in the political landscape, Tin Town is a powerful and compelling reminder of the power of young people to change the world.

Without the extravagance of large production budgets and with the help of a modest creative team, Coppen's brilliant storytelling has carried his work along. A reviewer in the National Arts Festival newspaper, *Cue*, wrote,

> Sometimes you can achieve miracles with a simple but potent idea, a small budget and a pocket full of creativity. Such is the case with Neil Coppen's *Tin Bucket Drum*, a wonderful mythical fable that returns to the festival to weave its mythical magic anew.

Conscious of the fact that his theatre writing is in constant competition with film and television, in an interview with Roel Twjinstra and Emma Durden he says:

> We have to attract and excite new audiences into our theatres, and to do this we have to compete with the relentlessly visual realms of film and television. It is for this reason that I often employ and reference cinematic devices in my plays. Working cinematically simply means that I am working in a storytelling vernacular that younger audiences have access to.[1]

---

1. Twjinstra, R and Durden, E. Ten Contemporary Directors / Neil Coppen. *Theatre Directing in South Africa: Skills and Inspirations.* Eds. Roel Twjinstra and Emma Durden. KwaZulu-Natal and Johannesburg: Twist Theatre Development Projects and Jacana Media, 2014: 14.

Tin Bucket Drum is a perfect example of that storytelling vernacular. Its rhythmic form and percussive beat speak to a generation that has grown up in tune with a musical background of hip hop, rap and RnB.

The play itself should resonate with so many young people in the world who are in revolt against the constrictions and constructions of the past and in search of a voice for the future.

Nandi's words towards the end of the play sum up that search as she communes with the spirit of her daughter:

> They taught me to never sing these songs.
> They made me leave your bedroom in silence
> each night.
> They made us forget our freedom.
> But you, you my child,
> taught us how to fight.

Neil Coppen's allegory allows us to reflect on the political landscape that we must so determinedly change if we are to offer the next generation a place anchored in social justice, hope, the freedom to dream and the creativity to tell stories, because that remains the most powerful tool with which we can celebrate our humanity.

Tin Bucket Drum

Questions with Neil Coppen

Dylan McGarry, educational sociologist and theatre maker, chats to Neil Coppen.

What inspired this story? Where and how was the initial story seed planted and what was it that compelled you to eventually sit down and write it?

I was in my early twenties and mostly working as an actor at the time. I had become increasingly frustrated with being a passive vehicle for telling other people's stories. At the time, the sorts of plays I was being cast in were mostly English and American ones. I was at a music concert in Durban and a friend of mine, Mike Mazzoni, who headed up a local percussive group called Interittmo Drummers, set me a challenge: to close my eyes during the performance and see if the drumming inspired any ideas for a theatrical collaboration. That night I closed my eyes during the drummers' performance and in the darkness was visited by the image of a small child marching triumphantly while banging a tin bucket drum. At the time I wasn't entirely sure why she was marching or who she was for that matter, but over the next few months the image and story percolated into what would eventually become one of my first plays: *Tin Bucket Drum*.

You could say the plays I write stem from a combination of my political curiosities and frustrations. When I look back at the South African zeitgeist at the time of writing: president Jacob Zuma was deeply entrenched in the arms deal debacle, Robert Mugabe was cracking down on neighbouring Zimbabwe, newspapers were full of harrowing stories of communities being bullied by governments to sign away their ancestral land to mining companies and the South African nation, ten years into democracy, seemed to be waking up to the fact that its rainbow ideals were fast disintegrating. All these threads seemed to combine, albeit allegorically, in the writing of the play.

The play is almost constructed like a ballad in its celebration of the life of a folkloric or mythical heroine.

Exactly. With the original cast and collaborators: Wake Mahlobo (percussionist), Ntando Cele (actress), Karen Logan (director) and myself, we set about composing the story text as one long narrative song (as one would an opera libretto) defined by a series of percussive movements, sounds, rhythmic motifs and refrains.

The Censor, for example, has a military marching drum that announces his arrival and departure each time. For Nomvula, the Little Drummer Girl, we settled on more organic tin and wood sounds; the heart-beats of the various town folks are denoted by recognisable and distinctive instruments/percussive surfaces. We used instruments to denote character just as Russian composer Sergei Prokofiev did with his *Peter and the Wolf* composition.

There's also a sort of homage to radio theatre in the way you staged the production by having the percussionist clearly visible on stage.

We referenced the Foley artists of old radio-dramas and films by lighting the percussionist on stage so that the audience is constantly aware of the source and origin of the play's soundtrack and effects. While the actress would mime the action on stage, the percussionist would orchestrate its exact sound in time to her choreography.

When these two layers work in seamless synergy, the effect is quite magical. I learnt with this play how much the audience like witnessing the mechanics of storytelling. Cinema, you could say, tries to conceal those mechanics but theatre tends to celebrate them.

There is a strong use of light and shadow in the design. Can you tell us more about the use of shadow in the design?

Again much of the design was born from the creative challenges we had thrown in our path in the devising of the work. I didn't imagine at first that I would need to consider things that could be packed down into the boot of a car for touring purposes. For example, the baobab tree is a central image in the story, but to physically build a tree to the scale I wanted would have been impossible for the reasons mentioned above. I discovered that when you shine a shadow light on a cut out of a baobab (40 cm high in our case) you could enlarge its shadow several metres behind on the wall of the theatre, thus achieving scale yet minimising expense and hassle. This worked for the Censor character, in the way we could manipulate and enlarge the performer's shadow to a monstrous scale. We spent weeks experimenting with various cardboard cut outs, gauzes, light sources and angles to get it all right.

You mentioned cinema earlier. People often call your work cinematic. In what way would you say this is true?

You could say I work cinematically in the way I liberally employ devices more common to film than the stage. For example, for the shadow puppetry, I employed small shadow tableaux scenes that dissolved in and out of the hessian screens to reveal shifts in time and location.

You could say I was working as a film director might, employing a cinematic long shot … establishing the scene (wide angle) before asking the audience to journey deeper into it with the actor.

So achieving the end visual results on stage comes from long periods of experimentation and collaboration?

Absolutely. Having time to play and improvise with lights in a dark space is integral to how my ideas for staging/ storytelling take shape. The simplest effects in theatre are often the most evocative and what's so wonderful about utilising shadow on stage is that the audience's imaginations are engaged and they are invited to play along with the story. The original stage version has been performed by three incredible women over the last decade, namely: Ntando Cele, Thuli Zuma and Mpume Mthombeni.

***Tin Bucket Drum* toured around South Africa and the world for over a decade. It received rave reviews in New York and a 2015 version (directed by Jade Bowers) has returned from an acclaimed run in Prague. What do you think it is about this story that has made it endure for so long?**

The thing I have learnt from my literary mentor-satirists, such as Jonathan Swift and George Orwell, is that human nature is tragically predictable and consistent. No matter how many centuries pass, or what continent we find ourselves writing from, we are likely to be commenting on the same patterns repeating themselves over and over again. Working in allegory means one never limits the story to an exact time and place because the themes of the story tend to outlast a single fleeting moment of time or history ... Orwell's *Animal Farm* is the perfect case in point.

I hoped *Tin Bucket Drum* would be universal in this way. I wanted it to speak closely to our ongoing reality here in South Africa and on the African continent yet, at the same time, appeal to audiences from across the globe that would just as easily be able to consider the story's ideas and concerns as their own.

It's a classic archetypal myth, told with imagination and heart, and I imagine audiences, in the age of excess and spectacle and interminable ongoing televised narratives, respond to its earnest simplicity the most.

Can you tell us about how you managed to get president Jacob Zuma to watch the production? You mentioned earlier he provided some of the inspiration for the Censor character.

As I mentioned at the beginning of the interview, the Zuma Arms deal controversy inspired some of the writing of this play. The Censor is very much a Mugabe/Zuma/Amin hybrid. It's the dream of any writer to have the object of one's barbs sit in their audience. So often we are accused as theatre makers of preaching to the converted and I really wanted to challenge this notion. There's also a valid criticism emerging in recent years that it's not the oppressed that need to be confronted with these sorts of stories but the oppressors themselves. How else can we attempt to subvert the status quo if we are not trying to prick the dormant empathetic consciences of those in power? So naturally I wanted president Zuma and his cronies to sit through a performance, but realistically never expected it to happen.

What happened?

In a twist of fate when I was recasting the production, Jacob Zuma's daughter Thuli Zuma, who is a trained and very accomplished actress, asked to audition. Karen Logan, the director, flew down to Cape Town and ended up auditioning Thuli in the president's residence, a grandiose boardroom with velvet curtains. Against any expectations she gave a courageous and convincing audition and seemed unfazed by the political nature of the piece and its rather unsubtle references to her presidential father. A week or so into our rehearsal, Zuma's personal assistant called with a request for him to attend the play.

What was that experience like?

I can only describe it as the most surreal evening at the theatre. We arrived to find helicopters circling, an army of police in bullet proof vests scouring the venue, sniffer dogs straining on leashes, more metal detectors than JFK airport post 9/11 and all the blue-light fanfare that accompanies JZ [Jacob Zuma] wherever he goes.

I sat behind the prez [president] throughout the performance, and I felt just like Hamlet, where he sets out to stage a play to catch the conscience of his uncle king Claudius, who during the re-enacted murder scene rises guiltily and flees the theatre yelling: 'Lights ... lights!'

Unlike Claudius, Zuma only shifted uncomfortably in his seat. Afterwards while posing on stage alongside his daughter for a photo op, I caught him wagging a finger at her and whispering through a grimace: 'You should have warned me before what this play was about!'

Scene 1. Shadow puppet detail of the Little Drummer Girl (Nomvula) on hessian screen. Loft Theatre, The Playhouse, Durban, 2010.
Photographer: Val Adamson

Scene 2. Mpume Mthombeni (Nandi) arrives in Tin Town to find a paradise ruined with rust. Kalk Bay Theatre, Cape Town, 2013.
Photographer: Jesse Kramer

Scene 4. Thuli Zuma (Nandi) sets eyes on the Little Drummer Girl (Nomvula) for the first time. Catalina Theatre, Durban, 2010.
Photographer: Colwyn Thomas

Scene 8. Mpume Mthombeni (Mkhulu) waits with her thirsty bucket raised to the sky. Kalk Bay Theatre, Cape Town, 2013.
Photographer: Jesse Kramer

Scene 8. Ntando Cele (Mkhulu) breaks the silence. Thomas More College, school performance, 2007.
Photographer: Xavier Vahed

Scene 10. Ntando Cele (Sangoma) accuses Nomvula of waking the ancestors. Thomas More College, school performance, 2007.
Photographer: Xavier Vahed

Scene 10. Mpume Mthombeni portrays the disapproving headmistress while percussionist Wake Mahlobo watches on. Kalk Bay Theatre, Cape Town, 2013.
Photographer: Jesse Kramer

Scene 13. Mpume Mthombeni (Nomvula) begins delivering water rations to the town. Kalk Bay Theatre, Cape Town, 2013.
Photographer: Jesse Kramer

Scene 13. Mpume Mthombeni (Nomvula) sleeps under the shadow baobab before the rains arrive. Kraine Theatre, New York, 2012.
Photographer: Neil Coppen

Scene 14. Shadow puppetry on hessian screens depicting the rhythmic revolution of Tin Town. Loft Theatre, The Playhouse, Durban, 2010.
Photographer: Val Adamson

Scene 14. Mpume Mthombeni (Censor) implores the angry masses to step back. Loft Theatre, The Playhouse Company, Durban, 2010.
Photographer: Val Adamson

Scene 14. Mpume Mthombeni's (Censor) ears bleed (kabuki style) from the revolutionary noise. Loft Theatre, The Playhouse Company, Durban, 2010.
Photographer: Val Adamson

Tin Bucket Drum:
the play script

Note on staging

The stage directions included in this text come from the original production. While the production is set in an unspecified African country its themes and concerns are universal and the author gives theatre-makers full permission to translate and adapt the narrative to suit relevant cultures and contexts.

Tin Bucket Drum is essentially a one-woman play but while the narrator figure has the task of bringing a variety of characters to life she is supported throughout by a percussionist, who sits to one side of the action.

The percussionist is surrounded by an array of traditional African percussive instruments as well as everyday objects, including tin teapots, plates and metal cutlery.

The percussionist and performer work together to bring the story to life, with the percussive soundtrack providing musical links and accompanying sound effects to orchestrate the performer's actions on stage. A wooden kitchen table is placed centre stage. Several rusty tin buckets encircle the playing space.

Three gauze screens provide the backdrop. When the play was originally staged these screens were employed to project a range of shadow play from behind and in front.

Although the play is divided into 16 mini-scenes, the storytelling should flow effortlessly from one location to the next.

---

*Note: The text is a combination of isiZulu and English. It is presented here mostly in its English form.

Scene 1

A celebration

The NARRATOR *takes her position centre stage. She is dressed in tattered white garments, her face painted with white clay. A red sash is tied around her waist.*

Eerie music plays. Drumming begins and builds. The scent of Impepho (traditional incense) fills the theatre. A rusted metal baobab tree cut out stands at the centre of the table and the low lighting angle casts imposing shadows of the tree upon the back screen.

NARRATOR: Once a year, on the day of her passing, we gather beneath the tree.

'Is it time?' the little ones ask, clutching their tin buckets in one hand, tugging their mothers' skirts with the other.

'Nearly time,' respond their parents.

'See the heavens heavy with the first rains.

Quickly, hang your bucket, it's good luck to be the first one.'

The elders lift the children up to the great branches of the baobab 'til it's full, bending beneath the weight of its tin bucket decorations.

Then wait … and wait.

Palms ready, feet poised.

The crowd whispering.

Anxious with anticipation.

Djembe percussion begins and builds and builds.

NARRATOR: She is coming … she is coming.

She is drumming, she is drumming.

'Is it time?'

'Nearly time.'
'Is it time?'
'Nearly time.'
Time … for the celebration!!

Drumming climaxes, then diminishes.

NARRATOR: She is coming.
She is coming.
She is drumming.
She is drumming.
Listen down the street.
She is dancing … She is dancing.
Hear the music in her heart.
Hear the music in her feet.
Bringing, she is bringing
the rain, she is bringing.
Listen in the wind.
Hear her singing.
She is singing.

Is it time?
Nearly time.
Is it time?
Nearly time … nearly time … nearly time …

The NARRATOR *shrinks into darkness.* PERCUSSION *culminates and fades.*

Scene 2

The journey

The stage is washed in moonlight. The NARRATOR *loads the table onto her back and walks in a weary circle, her body struggling beneath the weight of the table.*

NARRATOR: On a cold and starless night, through the desert came the stranger.

A woman by the name of Nandi, widowed by civil war. With a few belongings strung to her back and an unborn baby restless in her belly, she had escaped. The woman's husband had spoken of this place before: Tin Town. He had promised that after the war he would take her there, to that place where music was said to rattle over rooftops and into one's dreams. Where lullabies mingled in the evening breezes and each new day was met with a dance.

NARRATOR *now assumes the role of* NANDI, *offloading the table from her shoulders and placing her hands on her belly, comforting her unborn babe with reassuring whispers.*

NANDI: Nearly there ... nearly there.

See the lights of Tin Town, see them shining now like stars.

Listen to their music. They will bless you there.
Welcome you into the world with their drums.
Can you hear it, my little one?
Lalela [listen] ... *Lalela* [listen].

NANDI *listens, but there is silence.*

NARRATOR: The only drumming she could hear was her unborn child's impatient fists. Ready … restless … longing to dance free.

The PERCUSSIONIST *pounds three forceful beats on the djembe as* NANDI *collapses to the ground clutching her belly.*

NARRATOR: That morning Nandi arrived in Tin Town, but it was hardly the place described to her by her husband.

NANDI *rises, dusts herself off and notices a tin bucket on the other side of the stage. She rushes over to the bucket and raises it to her parched lips, she stops before drinking.*

NARRATOR: Here she was to find a paradise ruined with rust, its rivers dry, wells near empty. All hope turned to dust.

NANDI *turns the bucket upside down and sand pours out.*

NARRATOR: Above, the sun burnt fiercely in the sky. Stony faced soldiers lined the gravel road as a procession of black umbrellas shuffled past in ghostly silence. It was a silence that hovered over the whole town. Here no dogs dared to bark, birds were scared to sing. Even the clocks had stopped ticking.

The NARRATOR *resumes the role of* NANDI, *trying to attract the attention of the passersby. She rushes up and down the line begging for help, but the procession pushes past, oblivious.*

NANDI: Have you all lost your tongues?
Who has stolen your stories … your songs?
Who has silenced your drums?

As the NARRATOR, *she turns to the audience and pushes a finger forcefully to her lips.*

NARRATOR: Shhhhhhhhhhhhhhhhh!

Again, the defiant percussive heartbeat pounds [three times] and NANDI *collapses to the ground, holding her belly. From her whimpers it is clear that labour has begun.*

Lights fade.

NARRATOR: After the meeting, one of the village elders, Mkhulu, saw Nandi, doubled over in the dust, holding her belly and whispering … it is time … it is time. He took pity on her and welcomed her into his home.

Scene 3

Mkhulu's welcome

The NARRATOR *puts on a crumpled hat, transforming herself into the benevolent old man,* MKHULU, *who ushers* NANDI *into his home, all the while glancing suspiciously over his shoulder to ensure no one is watching.*

To indicate we are moving into an interior of a home, a window frame is projected on the shadow screen behind.

MKHULU [*In a frightened whisper*]: Woza … woza … woza … come … come in.

The old man shuts the door quietly behind him, dusting off surfaces as he goes. He places the table centre stage while untying the red sash and laying it over the table as a tablecloth. Although the room is sparse, it is clear that the old man takes enormous pride in his home. It would also seem from his enthusiasm that he has not entertained a guest here for many years.

Scene 4

A child is born

Lighting state changes with magical percussive accompaniment. The NARRATOR *now stands with her back to the audience.*

PERCUSSIONIST *sounds the heart beat (three times) as the* NARRATOR *slowly turns to face the audience, hands cradling a newborn child, which is represented here by the tablecloth formed into a bundle.*

NANDI *gazes adoringly at the cradled babe, her arms pulsating gently with the percussionist's heartbeats. A magical tinkling fills the space.*

NARRATOR: That evening the child was born.

Heartbeat percussion sounds again (three times). NANDI *steps forward, sharing the new arrival with her audience.*

NARRATOR: For the first time in 20 years a child was born. A child with a heartbeat that drummed loud and proud into the night without fear or hesitation. A child unafraid to rejoice in the sensations of her laughter, her tears and even though they managed to silence her voice [*beat*] they could never quite silence the beating of her heart.

Heartbeat percussion sounds again (three times) and NANDI *rocks the child gently to sleep.*

NARRATOR: The old man took her in his arms.

The NARRATOR *transforms into the old man, reaching over and tenderly taking the baby/cloth in his trembling arms. He smiles and whispers warmly …*

MKHULU: Ahhh, Nomvula. I have been waiting for her. The Little Drummer Girl … she has come. But it is not safe for her here, Nandi. You must take her away from this town. They will try to silence her, try to silence her little heart!

NARRATOR: But Nandi shook her head sadly.

Back to NANDI.

NANDI: There are no places of peace left. I'm tired of running now, always running, searching for a better life when it does not exist. This town is my last hope. Please, Mkhulu … please let us stay.

NARRATOR: The old man agreed, but on one condition.

Back to MKHULU, *insistent and pleading.*

MKHULU: We should not, must not, cannot let the Silent Sir and his government hear about this child!

Scene 5

Awakening

NARRATOR: So Nandi agreed to keep her baby hidden and for months she rested in the shadows of Mkhulu's shack.

NANDI *unravels the red tablecloth and uses it now as a shawl, worn over her shoulders, to conceal the child she cradles in her arms.*

NARRATOR: Until she could not bear it any longer, could not bear to keep little Nomvula a secret, when all she wanted was to show her off to the rest of the world.

NANDI *emerges, a little tentatively, from the shadows and begins to journey into Tin Town.*

NARRATOR: That is how the first miracle happened. While she was taking a walk into the centre of town, the people she passed stopped what they were doing, stirred out of their silent spell by an unmistakable rhythm ... [*The* PERCUSSIONIST *sounds his heartbeat drum three times*] ... each person moving towards the stranger and her bundle and placing an inquisitive ear to the child's heart ...

The NARRATOR *mimes a curious stranger craning an ear towards the child's noisy breast. The* PERCUSSIONIST *sounds the heart beat (three times), to which the stranger reacts with a mixture of horror and delight.*

... Then placing trembling hands to their own.

The NARRATOR, *demonstrating the reaction of the townsfolk, holds a tentative hand to her heart. As it makes contact she finds her hands jumping in time to the percussive beat (three times).*

We see the NARRATOR *in quick succession leaping among four townsfolk performing the same action.*

During this sequence each heartbeat is scored differently. Some are light and tinny, others deep and booming. The percussionist employs a different African drum or percussive sound for each character, so when played together they form a beautiful and chaotic cacophony.

Lights fade as an ominous military drum sounds from offstage. Where joy is etched into the face of the last participant in this game, it quickly turns to an expression of outright terror.

Scene 6

Sermon

The wooden table is rolled forward to form a podium and the NARRATOR, wearing a military hat, slinks into the light as the CENSOR.

The use of low floor lighting casts a looming shadow on the screens.

The CENSOR speaks in evangelical rhyme, gesticulating wildly and pounding fists on the podium for additional emphasis.

CENSOR: Good citizens, I have summoned you all to this urgent meeting, for it has come to my attention that once again the silence has been disturbed by a heart's … beat … beat … beating!

At each utterance of 'beat', 'beat', 'beating' the CENSOR bangs his clenched fist on the podium and the PERCUSSIONIST accompanies it with a drum.

CENSOR: And it's this, this beat … beat … beating.
This unlawful silence-defeating din!
That has caused you all to stop
with blatant disregard and in defiant fashion.
Awaken and regard your own false and foolish passion!
Good people of Tin Town.
Who has led you such depths of sin?
Who has unleashed the tyrannical beat,
the rhythmic devil …

The PERCUSSIONIST, *growing a bit cocky, rolls his military drum for emphasis. The* CENSOR *shoots him a stern glance.*

CENSOR: … that sounds and pounds within?
　　　　Who is it that sits amongst us today … Eh?

The CENSOR *scans the audience suspiciously.*

CENSOR: Pulls you into this depravity?
　　　　Who dares to challenge the Almighty's
　　　　sacred and silent decree?
　　　　Who is it that chooses to threaten this state?
　　　　Defy our leader?
　　　　Place our sacred silence in danger!

Another fist on the podium, accompanied by a drumbeat.

CENSOR: We must find the courage, good people.
　　　　To weed out the culprit.
　　　　Sniff out the stranger.

The CENSOR *puts his nose in the air and sniffs rudely. He stops and glares into the crowd.*

CENSOR: Wena [Who is it]? Woza [Come here].

He motions with an extended finger for the culprit to come forward from the audience. A dreadful silence as NANDI *offers the child. He takes it carefully (in mime) and holds his ear to the babe's breast. A heartbeat pounds proudly (three times). He glances up at his congregation, appalled.*

CENSOR: This….this…. child?
　　　　How can something so small, so harmless, make
　　a racket so awful?

Such an insolent hearbeat in one so young is not just unnatural … it's unlawful!

It's shameful, a disgrace, when children born into Tin Town do not obey the rules, the laws.

When children do not know their place!

He bangs his fist on 'place'. Side lights snap as the CENSOR *changes into* NANDI *(taking off hat), turning her back to the audience and pleading, with outstretched arms.*

NANDI [*desperate, her voice wavering*]: I will teach her then. Give me time! She's barely four weeks old. She has much to learn about the ways of your town.

Then switches back into the unimpressed CENSOR, *glaring disdainfully down at her.*

CENSOR: In order for this child to stay,
From us all, she must be hidden away
and with each and every passing day,
offer her a hand – strong and stern.
Guide her along her silent way.
I recommend then … that to make a start.
You crush the unlawful rhythms in her soul.

Bellowing from the podium.
Silence the beating of her heart!

He bangs his fist a final three times on the podium. Military drumming begins as the lights fade on the scene.

Scene 7

Silent confinement

We move back to Mkhulu's shack. The shadow of a window frame appears on the centre screen.

NARRATOR: So the Little Drummer Girl's mother was forced to keep her hidden in the safety and silence of Mkhulu's back room. Here they padded the floors with grass mats so that the girl would not be tempted by the rhythm in her own footsteps; sealed up the windows and doors, removed all objects from the house …

The NARRATOR *moves around the house, miming the removal of a variety of offending objects. As she does this, the* PERCUSSIONIST *orchestrates each sound. This is done in perfect unison.*

NARRATOR: Cutlery.

The NARRATOR *mimes opening a drawer and collecting all the cutlery, then tossing it aside. The* PERCUSSIONIST *provides the sound.*

NARRATOR: Tin.

The NARRATOR *mimes throwing out tin items.* PERCUSSIONIST *provides the clatter.*

NARRATOR: Bottle caps.

The NARRATOR *mimes gathering bottle caps.* PERCUSSIONIST *provides the sound from the actual objects.*

NARRATOR: And plates.

The NARRATOR *mimes sliding the plates off a shelf.*
PERCUSSIONIST *provides the sound using tin plates. After*
the final tin plate hits the floor, the NARRATOR, *nerves*
frayed, turns back to the audience and whispers.

NARRATOR: Anything that might inspire forbidden
rhythmic activities. [*Pause.*] Eight years would pass
like this. Eight long years of this silent confinement.

The NARRATOR *sits on the edge of the table (the red*
tablecloth is now doubling as a bedspread), assuming the
character of NOMVULA, *the Little Drummer Girl. Her legs*
dangle awkwardly off the edge.

NARRATOR [*mischievously*]: But she found a way. She
always found a way to keep the rhythm in her heart
alive. You see, she had kept a secret beneath her
pillow.

The NARRATOR *removes something from underneath the*
pillow and holds it out for the audience to inspect.

NARRATOR: a box of matches, the one her mother had
used to light her bedside candle. Well, at night, when
all of Tin Town was asleep, the child would shake the
box, rattling the matches.

NOMVULA *produces an (imaginary) box of matches. She*
hops off the table and rises on tiptoe to peep through the
window, ensuring that no guards are patrolling. Once she
is certain that it is safe, she begins to tap the box musically
against her chest.

The PERCUSSIONIST *creates the rattling matchbox rhythms*

as NOMVULA *dances in defiant circles around the room.*
She then moves to the table and folds back the red cloth, as
though she is climbing into bed.

NARRATOR: Then, falling into a deep, musical sleep,
she would dream. The same dream over and over.
Even though it had not rained in Tin Town for 20
years, in her dreams she could hear it … [*pause*] … a
raindrop striking the bottom of a tin bucket.

For this sequence a few miniature tin buckets are attached to
a spinning mobile device set downstage. The NARRATOR
spins the mobile gently and, lit by the floor lights, the
whirling shadows of the buckets are amplified on the screen.

Shadow buckets dance magically around the room as the
NARRATOR *spins in circles amongst them. The*
PERCUSSIONIST *plays on the bottom of an upturned tin*
bucket to create the falling rain effect/music.

Lights slowly fade.

Scene 8

Mkhulu's story

As lights go up again we see NOMVULA *sitting on the edge of her bed and whispering to* MKHULU.

NOMVULA: Pssst … Psst … Mkhulu, please tell me a story. Tell me of a time when people were free to sing and dance. How did they sing? How did they dance? Show me. Please show me. [*Pause.*] Why must they lock me in this room, hide me away from the rest of the town? I have done nothing wrong Mkhulu … I only listened to the beating of my heart.

She climbs off the bed and retrieves MKHULU'S *hat, placing it on her head.*

NARRATOR: The old man shook his head sadly, distant memories dancing in his eyes.

NARRATOR *now assumes the role of doddery* MKHULU, *preparing to tell his story.*

MKHULU: My father founded this town on a dream … a dream of a desert, a tin bucket and a rain drop. He came here with plans to build Africa's first tin bucket factory. Buckets that could be used by villagers to transport water during the dry season. Buckets that could be distributed to all the villages across the continent. With the money they made from this tin bucket factory they built this town, Tin Town.

The PERCUSSIONIST *begins to build tin music into the old man's narrative.*

MKHULU: While the men would work in the mines, the women would beat the tin into buckets at the factory. All the time singing ... singing ... singing.

The tin sounds build into an infectious drumming.

MKHULU: Singing while they worked. From out of the din, the clanging of tin, they created songs, praise to the ancestors, who responded by sending the rains each year. As children we used to wait ... wait with our thirsty buckets raised to the sky.

MKHULU *raises a tin bucket anxiously to the heavens in the hope of catching a precious rain drop. He waits expectantly for a few seconds but nothing comes.*

MKHULU: But I was just a boy then. Just a boy when the men from the Silent Sir government first arrived.

He lowers his bucket. Ominous music and military drumming fill the space.

We revert to a flashback. MKHULU *disappears behind the centre gauze screen before reappearing through it as the* CENSOR. *This time he dissolves menacingly through the gauze, back-lit and resembling a monstrous Kafkaesque cockroach. He is accompanied by frenzied percussion that weaves in and out of his hypnotic speech.*

CENSOR*:* Good citizens of Tin Town ... I bring good news.

The way of the Silent Sir, you can't refuse.

A life free of all this rhythmic sin ...

Free from the persuasive rhythms that tempt you from this tin.

Rhythm!

Making monsters from the mundane.

Stirring ancestors from their graves to inspire
REVOLUTION.

Pollution!

Rhythm …

A sacred relative to ritual.

Inspiring, unlawful, ungodly behaviours …

Dancing … Drinking … Promiscuity …
Prostitution!

Rhythm …

That devours, consumes and ravages.

Obscuring the mind.

Turning you into wild, undignified savages!

Good people, weed out your instruments of mass
disturbance.

Rid this town of its cultural plague.

Burn the story books, the dictionaries, the drums.

Silence the laughter … the whispers … the songs.

For the Almighty Silent Sir – HE HEARS ALL!

Silence is the way to your salvation.

Without it you fall.

*A beat as he regains composure, changing his tone, oozing with
insincerity.*

Good people …

To drive the devil and his music from your
town …

To silence the noise in your hearts …

You must first close the mine and bucket factory
down.

*He bangs his fists three times (with percussive accompaniment)
and the lights fade.*

Lights up again on the old man, MKHULU, *resuming his tale in front of the screens. His tin bucket is still raised expectantly to the heavens.*

MKHULU [*shaking his head sadly, his voice frail*]: A dreadful silence descended over this town. That year we waited … waited with our buckets raised to the sky, but not a drop fell. No, it has not rained since. [*Pause.*] These men of power thought they could silence us; thought they could confiscate our music. I was young and foolish then, and so I fought. Fought with the only weapon I possessed … the mightiest weapon of all: my drumsticks.

MKHULU *produces an imaginary pair of drumsticks and hits them together, with the* PERCUSSIONIST *providing the sound.*

MKHULU: I played on tables …

He mimes each act of rhythmic defiance as the PERCUSSIONIST *orchestrates the drumming on a variety of different surfaces.*

MKHULU: Tree trunks … water drums … dustbin lids and doorways. Not only using my sticks but my hands … my tongue … my fingers … my feet. Where there was silence I broke it! [*A silence.*] Which is why it didn't take long for them to find me. [*Pause. His voice cracks and tears well in his eyes.*] They broke my hands so I could no longer play my drum, broke my legs so I would never dance again. They locked me in jail for ten long, silent years. It was here, in this silence, that my soul, my voice, my rhythm deserted me forever.

The lights fade on the defeated MKHULU.

Scene 9

Integration

Lights snap up on the NARRATOR *setting the dinner table at Mkhulu's house.*

NARRATOR: On the Little Drummer Girl's tenth birthday her mother, Nandi, decided it was time for her to be integrated back into the silent society.

The NARRATOR, *playing the little girl, sits on an upturned bucket peering over the table-top. There is an effective trick of perspective and scale created by the smallness of the bucket in relation to the table ledge.*

NARRATOR: That's right, she was going to sit with Nandi and Mkhulu at the dinner table. First her mother handed her a plate. Then her own knife and fork.

She mimes carefully receiving the plate and utensils, accompanied by the PERCUSSIONIST'S *carefully judged sound effects.*

NARRATOR: That's when she felt it. An itch in her finger tips … an itch that no scratching could ease; an itch that spread through her body like wildfire.

The LITTLE DRUMMER GIRL *(with support from the* PERCUSSIONIST *throughout the scene) drums furiously on the table top with imaginary eating utensils before throwing them back down again, afraid. Silence. She glances apologetically over at her mother and then at the old man, before reaching again for her knife and fork, determined to keep the rhythm suppressed.*

25

Once again she is overcome by the need. She drums wildly on her tin plate, then rises, dancing to the rhythm she has created. She clicks her cutlery together defiantly.

The NARRATOR *hops to the left of the table and portrays* NANDI, *who has succumbed to the music and risen, shaking a salt cellar in time to the beat, then switches back to the* DRUMMER GIRL *(centre) then to* MKHULU, *who gleefully rises and hits a teapot with a teaspoon, chuckling all the while. Then back to the* DRUMMER GIRL *in the centre, who plays furiously on her plate. Eventually the dance and music reach a climax.*

NARRATOR: When the dance ended the three collapsed, but Nandi shook her head in sadness.

As NANDI.

NANDI [*shaking her head, perturbed*]: Ai … ai, is there no end to this rhythm? No *muthi* to cure this madness?

Scene 10

Problem child

A djembe drum links the following montage.

NARRATOR: And so, the following day, they paid an urgent visit to the town doctor, who, after pressing his stethoscope to the Little Drummer Girl's chest …

NARRATOR *assumes role of the doctor, holding an imaginary stethoscope to the child's heart. Drums pound the heart beat (three times).*
    … chased them away, frightened.

She moves to another point on the stage and, using an upturned bucket as a seat, becomes the SANGOMA [traditional healer].
    The redundant *Sangoma* on the outskirts of the town couldn't help much either …

SANGOMA [*frightened, swats away the spirits that surround him*]: Ai, there is no *muthi* to cure this! She is born with the song of the ancestors, making the spirits restless, waking the ghosts with the beating of her heart. She is a danger to the silence, making me see things I long to see but am forbidden to. You must take her away for your own safety and mine. *Hambani* [Get out]! *Hambani*!

The SANGOMA *rises, shooing them out of his hut.*

NARRATOR: So the girl's mother was left with little option but to send her off on her first day of school and, for a few weeks, it seemed a solution had been found. Miss Khumalo, the headmistress, reported that …

The narrator assumes the role of MISS KHUMALO, *scribbling on the desk as though filling in a report card. The* PERCUSSIONIST *creates the sound of the scribbling pen in time to the teacher's hand movements on the table.*

MISS KHUMALO: … the Little Drummer Girl excels in her studies …

She puts an exaggerated full stop, which is punctuated by the PERCUSSIONIST.
   … hungry for every ounce of knowledge her teacher has to offer.

Marks another full stop.
   She has earned no noise demerits and there have been no reports of rhythmic disturbances!

She adds an exclamation mark, with percussive accompaniment.

NARRATOR: That was before the terrible twins, two of her classmates, grew jealous of the attention the teacher devoted to the new pupil.

An ominous drumming starts. The NARRATOR *assumes the character of the disgruntled* TWINS, *sitting on the front of the table, arms folded sulkily.*

TWINS: No! We cannot let her popularity grow. Our minds are made up, the Little Drummer Girl must GO!

NARRATOR: The following break the twins invited her to join them in a game, a game they hoped would help unleash her dreadful secret.

The NARRATOR *takes a tin bucket from the circumference of the stage and spills sand across the playing space. She crouches down and sketches hopscotch squares in it with her finger.*

NARRATOR: First, the twins demonstrated, careful not to arouse the attention of Miss Khumalo.

One of the TWINS *demonstrates on the hopscotch squares.*

TWINS: 1 [*kunye*] … 2 [*kubili*] … 3 [*kuthathu*]. *Empushe* [go] … *empushe* [go].

TWIN ONE *tries to push* NOMVULA *into the game.*

NARRATOR: But Nomvula knew better, she turned to leave, but they shoved her back to the first square!

The narrator demonstrates NOMVULA'S *action, hovering over the first hopscotch square, tentative at first, before taking the first leap. Each hop becomes more energetic, eventually culminating in a wild, unbridled dance.* PERCUSSION *marks the sound of her feet hitting the ground.* NOMVULA *dances as though possessed.*

NARRATOR: Soon all the other children followed in Nomvula's footsteps, the whole playground erupting in a musical chaos.

NOMVULA *beckons to the other children.*

NOMVULA: *Wozani.* [Come]. *Wozani.*

The alternate floor lights create replica shadows on the gauze screens behind the dancing girl, creating the effect of more and more children joining her in the dance.

NARRATOR: Miss Khumalo, enraged at the sight, dragged the child by the ear and flung her into the classroom.

Drum rolls.

MISS KHUMALO: You will now write a ten-page essay explaining why rhythm is the work of the devil.

NARRATOR *sits at the school desk/table as* NOMVULA. *She mimes taking out two pencils from her case. She feels the itch and tries to suppress it, but it pulses through her entire body. She raises her pencils in the air then brings them down on the desk lid, playing a final defiant rhythm before tossing them aside.* NOMVULA *peers sheepishly up at the headmistress who stands over her.*

Lights fade on the image.

Scene 11

Legacy

NARRATOR: That afternoon Nomvula was expelled from the school. When she arrived home she found Mkhulu ill in bed. The town doctor, who had visited earlier that day, said it was unlikely he would live to see the end of the week.

The NARRATOR, *putting the hat on, assumes the voice and character of the frail old man, using the table as the bed. The red sash table cloth covers his legs. The shack window appears on the central screen behind him. The scene is lit in soft twilight colours.*

MKHULU [*comforting the child, who weeps at his bedside*]: Come come, don't cry little one. Don't cry. I am old now, it is my time to go. I am leaving to join the spirit world, to rally support there for you all. I will return in whatever way I can to help you in the silent struggle. [*Coughs.*] I have a gift to for you.

MKHULU *reaches under his bed and retrieves a pair of (imaginary) drumsticks. He holds them ceremoniously up to the light.*

UMHULU [*whispering*]: See, my drumsticks. I've kept these hidden for many years. [*Pause.*] The future does not lie in these drumsticks, my child, but in what YOU choose to do with them … use them carefully. [*He hands them to the girl.*] You will know when the time is right. How will you know, my child? [*Smiles tenderly at her for a final time.*] By listening.

MKHULU *removes his hat and holds it over his breast.*
We hear his heartbeat weaken (three times, scored by
PERCUSSION), *then stop. The movement of the hat up and*
down on his chest illustrates his slowing heart. He sighs a
final breath before surrendering his body. The hat falls to the
ground.

Lights fade.

Percussive link plays into next scene.

Scene 12

Rehabilitation

The NARRATOR *appears from various points behind the central table, peeping out as though from behind doorways and portraying a chorus of gossiping town members.*

NEIGHBOUR 1: It's the work of the devil!
She's an incarnation of evil.
Breaking our silence
with that rhythmic upheaval.

NEIGHBOUR 2: Mmmmm ... I've heard her before.
Tapping on fences.
Rattling tins in the shed.
This child has demons.
Tormenting her heart.
Tormenting her head.

NEIGHBOUR 3: She's Mad.
She's Distressed.
She's Wicked.
She's Possessed.

The neighbours chatter wildly as military drums sound and the CENSOR *rises menacingly at his podium (the table).*

CENSOR: Good people, calm yourselves ... calm yourselves.
I have decided that it would be only fair
in the interest of ALL of our safety
to remove this Nomvula from her mother's care.
It is now the responsibility of this state
to aid her in a sufficient recovery.
In other words ....

> With watchful eye and beady ear
> Rehabilitate!

He searches the crowd for NANDI *and her daughter. When he
spots them he extends an accusatory, beckoning finger.*
> Wena … Woza!

NOMVULA, *accompanied by her trembling mother, steps
forward. The* PERCUSSIONIST *notes their approaching
footsteps. The* CENSOR *eyes them up and down with disgust.*

CENSOR: After much consideration …
> Deliberation …
> Procrastination!
> It has been decided that the child is to be sent
away.
> Made to sleep by the well on the outskirts of the
town.
> Each day she will be forced to carry out an
arduous form of community service.
> She will be made to do this until the first rain
falls.

The CENSOR *turns into* NANDI, *taking off his military hat
and turning his back on the audience.*

NANDI [*pleading*]: But it has not rained in 20 years. She's
only a child … my only child.

Back to the CENSOR *at the podium.*

CENSOR: We must stop her before she commits further
sin.
> Taps one more pencil.
> Rattles one more tin.

Stop her before she's allowed to strike one more unruly blow.

My mind has been made ...

The Little Drummer Girl must go!

The CENSOR *bangs his fist three times on the podium before shrinking back into the darkness. Military drums sound and the lights fade on the image.*

Scene 13

Community service

Magical tinkling of a tin wind chime is heard.

We now move to the wells on the outskirts of town.

The cut out of the baobab tree is placed near one of the downstage floor lights, casting an enlarged shadow version of itself onto the front gauze screen.

NOMVULA *enters, taking in the alien surroundings. She lays a grass mat at the base of the shadow tree.*

NARRATOR: Nomvula was banished to sleep beneath the great baobab. During the day she would work at the wells. At first light she would rise, to lower bucket after bucket into the endless hole. Sometimes, when leaning over the well, she would hear her heartbeat echoing back at her …

NOMVULA *lowers an imaginary rope into a tin bucket placed at the edge of the stage. She stops and leans in, listening intently. Her heartbeat pounds (three times) and echoes in the well.*

NARRATOR: … giving her strength to face each day.

The NARRATOR *places a branch across her shoulders. It has tin buckets dangling from either side like a yoke. She starts to pace wearily back and forth on the same spot. The water in the buckets weighs heavily on her little shoulders. Music accompanies her journey.*

NARRATOR: Then she would begin the long walk into Tin Town, delivering water rations to the people's doorsteps. On these days the town had nothing better to do than line the streets and laugh at her. The children from school, pointing and pulling faces. Back and forth … back and forth … back and forth … days passed … weeks … months … back and forth … back and forth. One day, while she was out on the road, she cried out to the sun for help.

NARRATOR as **NOMVULA** [*gazing up to the heavens*]: Please, sun, help me by making your days shorter, your shade longer, your light softer.

NARRATOR: But the sun only frowned more angrily upon her.

NOMVULA: Then please, road, guide me away from this town. Take me to a place where my heart may beat freely again.

NARRATOR: But the road responded by twisting and turning like a snake; growing humps and bumps to make her task even more trying. With each tin bucket load the Little Drummer Girl began to curse the rhythm that had sent her to this forsaken place.

NOMVULA *unloads the bucket yoke from her shoulders and kneels down on the grass mat beneath the imposing shadow of the tree.*

NARRATOR: Each night she would attempt to keep the rhythm in her heart alive by rattling her box of matches. But the nights had grown cold and she was forced to use her matches to light her bedside fire instead.

NOMVULA *kneels on the mat and looks up into the sky, hands clasped, appealing to* MKHULU *and her ancestors.*

NOMVULA: Help me, Mkhulu. Help me to keep the rhythm in my heart alive. The longer you are away, the quieter it becomes. You said I should listen to my heart, and I do. It tells me one thing now.

She holds her hand to her breast and the PERCUSSIONIST *sounds the heart beat (three times).*

NOMVULA: The silence must be broken.

She raises her eyes expectantly to the heavens.

NARRATOR: But the heavens remained silent and the Little Drummer Girl, feeling betrayed by the ancestors, wished she could tear out her noisy heart and throw it to the bottom of the well; wished that, like the other children, she had a tin heart instead. That night, as she lit her fire, she watched her final match burn out.

She takes out an imaginary matchbox and lights a match, watching it fizzle out. Lights fade when the match burns out. NOMVULA *is swallowed up by the darkness.*

NARRATOR: Just like the box, she was silent and empty.

She curls up onto the mat and cries.

Scene 14

Revolution

The PERCUSSIONIST *creates the sound of a single raindrop striking the bottom of a tin bucket. At first the drops are tentative, but they gradually increase until there is a downpour.* NOMVULA *wakes and rises excitedly, extending her hands, then her tongue. She rejoices in the coolness of the water on her parched skin.*

Music underscores the sequence.

NARRATOR: The drought was breaking. Delighted by the sound, the girl began to hang the remaining buckets from the branches of the great baobab.

The NARRATOR *hangs miniature tin buckets on the baobab tree. Light casts an amplified shadow version on the gauze behind. The sound of rain hitting the bottoms of multiple tin buckets fills the space.*

NARRATOR: The tree began to drum its own tin bucket tune.

She takes a bucket filled with water and washes her face clean. The white clay washes away and for the first time we see her. She rises, dancing, stamping her feet into freshly formed puddles, raising her hands skyward.

NARRATOR: That night, after collecting every bucket she could find, she sneaked into the town, hanging her buckets above doorways … along fences … from lampposts … telephone poles … trees.

NOMVULA *rolls up her grass mat then rushes around the stage collecting the buckets and placing them at intervals around the playing space.*

NARRATOR: By the time she had finished, the whole of Tin Town was covered with them. After preparing herself with Mkhulu's drum sticks, a tin bucket drum strung around her neck, she took her place on a nearby hill.

NARRATOR *disappears behind the screen and is now seen as a dancing shadow, growing as she marches toward the light source.*

The PERCUSSIONIST'S *djembe drumming builds triumphantly into her speech.*

NARRATOR: The rain clouds, gathering behind her as if an army preparing its defences.
Thunder rolls.
Lightning flashes, tin bucket blue.
Rain falling, softly, slowly.
Pitter-patter, pitter-patter.
Then pouring.
Tin bucket drums pounding,
Finally she is here.
The child … has come.

The NARRATOR *moves to the front of the stage. As the lights rise she is lying on the table as if tucked up in bed.*

Drumming is building all the time.

NARRATOR: One by one the members of the town were shaken from their beds.

Then is a loud bang on the drum. She wakes afraid and scrambles under the table.

NARRATOR: Many hid beneath dining room tables, thinking the wrath of the Silent Sir had brought the sky crashing down.

She now uses the table to make a door, peering out from behind it.

NARRATOR: Only once they plucked up enough courage to peep beyond their doors did they find themselves caught in the trance, dancing out onto the street.

The drumming takes hold of her – possessed, she dances free, joining the procession.

The NARRATOR *takes on the role of* NOMVULA, *marching centre stage.*

NARRATOR: The *Sangoma* ... the doctor ... the headmistress and the nuns. The terrible twins and nosey neighbours. There wasn't a single person from the town who did not join in.

NARRATOR *marches proudly centre state. Music continues to build.*

NARRATOR: The Silent Sir guard reserves rushed forward, guns pointed, but the music was too powerful now. One by one, they dropped their weapons and picked up tin drums instead. All along the way the crowd grew bigger and bigger; the drumming louder and louder; the song stronger and stronger.

She marches around to the SILENT SIR'S *headquarters (the table).*

NARRATOR: Until they arrived outside the Silent Sir's headquarters, where they broke down the doors and stormed the building, demanding that the Censor step forward and explain himself!

She kicks down the table and marches into the CENSOR'S *office.*

The table is turned back on its feet to become the CENSOR'S *desk. The drumming stops.*

NARRATOR: But there was no sign of him. Only an empty office. Paperwork strewn across his desk.

The NARRATOR *empties a bucket onto one of the tables and a stack of paperwork spills out and scatters over the table and the stage. The* NARRATOR *takes a moment to rummage through the papers. Eventually her eyes fall on a document, which she scans before climbing onto the table and silencing the crowd and the drumming with a gesture.*

NOMVULA [*shouting over the noise and clutching the document*]: *Bakwethu* [Revolutionaries]! *Bakwethu*! It seems our poverty, suffering, silence has been in vain. All this time we have been robbed of our rhythm, our freedom, our rain and for what? What, I ask you? This paperwork proves that dirty deals were made underhand. The Tin Mine competitors from abroad bribed the Censor to close down our mines, while allowing theirs to expand!

The crowd's drumming climaxes furiously and she calms them once again.

NOMVULA: Rise … Rise, soldiers of the tin bucket drum.
Sing … Sing, children of the restless tongue.
Take back your hands … voices … stamping feet.
Take back your furious hearts
and let them beat … beat … beat!

The NARRATOR *jumps off table and puts on the* CENSOR'S *military hat. The* CENSOR *re-enters the playing space, clutching his ears and appalled at the disruption. He pushes through the crowd aggressively. The drumming intensifies.*

CENSOR: Silence … Silence … Silence!

He turns to the PERCUSSIONIST *and yells once more.*

Silence!

The PERCUSSIONIST *stops briefly, before resuming his beat. The* CENSOR *paces the stage like a wounded animal in a cage, roaring, seething.*

CENSOR: The truth is out. The Silent Sir was a figment of your foolish imaginations.

Drumming increases, pushing him backwards.

CENSOR: I created this myth to protect YOU!

As the mob's drumming closes in once again, the CENSOR *tries to placate them.*

CENSOR: To save you from this godforsaken noise!

Again, the crowd's drumming intensifies. The CENSOR, *trapped by the noise, clutches his ears in agony. He releases a terrible moan and, in an image reminiscent of Kabuki theatre, pulls two red ribbons (streams of blood) from a device concealed in his hat. The effect is that of his ears bleeding.*

CENSOR [*ranting*]: Rescue your souls from the clutches of those rhythmic demons. Good people, do not be fooled for the Devil [*pointing at* NOMVULA], *uSathane* walks amongst you today. I will not watch the sacred silence I have fought so long to preserve be destroyed by… a … a … heartbeat!

He thumps his foot three times [*scored by* PERCUSSION] *on the stage, trying to regain control.*

CENSOR: SILENCE MUST BE RESTORED!

The CENSOR, *demented and raging, clasps his hands in the shape of a pistol. The drumming slows as he lowers the weapon menacingly towards the audience. The* PERCUSSIONIST *creates the sharp and sudden crack of a bullet.*

A tin bucket hits the ground with a terrible thud.

Blackout.

Scene 15

Lullaby

There is an extended silence.

Lights up on NANDI, *cradling the body of* NOMVULA [red cloth] *in her arms. She begins singing softly, her voice trembling. Tears overcome her.*

*THIS song is an English translation of the original isiZulu.

NANDI: They taught me to never sing these songs.
　　They made me leave your bedroom in silence
　each night.
　　They made us forget our freedom.
　　But you, you my child
　　taught us how to fight.

　　Now I shall sing.
　　Sing you your first lullaby.
　　Sing you to sleep.
　　Sing you goodbye.

　　Sing now, the rains have come.
　　Sing for this new morning.
　　The struggle that you fought.
　　The struggle that you won.

　　Sing you your first lullaby.
　　Sing you to sleep.
　　Sing you goodbye.

NANDI *places her ear to the child's heart. For the final time the* PERCUSSIONIST *creates the sound of the heart slowing, softening, then stopping.*

Lights fade.

Scene 16

Rebirth

NARRATOR *begins to tie the cloth around her and rises to meet the audience. Music underscores.*

NARRATOR: It was said that later that afternoon the Drummer Girl's spirit left the town dancing … dancing from out of her mother's arms to where the ancestors and Mkhulu were waiting to receive her. Dancing over table tops … roof tops. High above the town and into the stars. [*Pause.*] The rain came every year after that and it wasn't long before the mines and tin bucket factory re-opened. The Censor was never seen again. It was said that he was chased from the town by the people's drumming, a drumming that would never again be silenced. [*Pause.*] The Little Drummer Girl was never forgotten. To this day it is still a tradition for the children of the town to cover its trees with tin buckets. They do this so that during the first rains they may hear the Drummer Girl dancing past their windows. You may hear her too if you listen carefully …

PERCUSSIONIST *begins to play the same beat on the djembe that accompanied the narrator's chant in the prologue.*
NARRATOR *resumes the position she started with.*

NARRATOR: She is coming … she is coming.
She is drumming, she is drumming.
'Is it time?'
'Nearly time.'
'Is it time?
'Nearly time'
'Look', one of the elders cries.

'She comes! She comes!'
Ears … eyes … hearts to the skies.
Listen.
Listen.
Listen to her drums!

Drums roll furiously.

NARRATOR: Thunder rolls.
Lightning flashes: tin bucket blue.
As she rolls her drumsticks across the heavens.
Rain falling, softly, slowly,
Pitter-patter, pitter-patter.
Then pouring.
Tin bucket drums pounding,
Finally she is here.
The child has returned.

Drumming climaxes. Lights fade.

Printed and bound by CPI Group (UK) Ltd, Croydon, CR0 4YY

14/04/2025

14656909-0001